PRESENTATION TOOLKIT

Unit Transparencies
Latin America

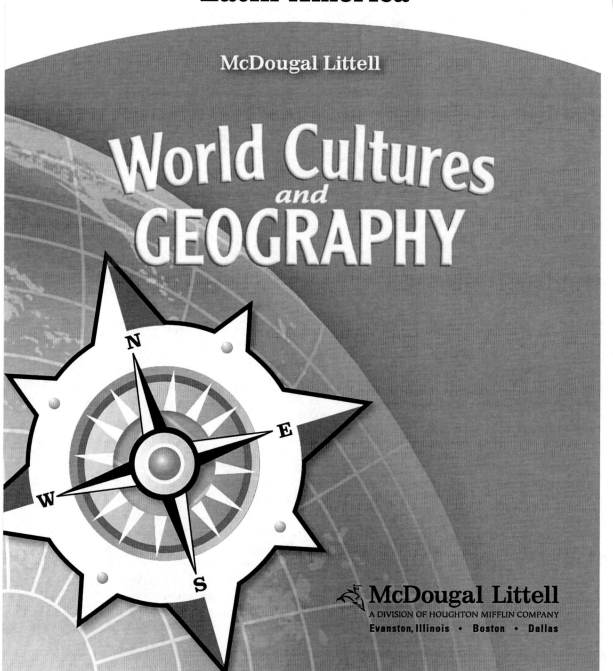

McDougal Littell

World Cultures *and* GEOGRAPHY

McDougal Littell
A DIVISION OF HOUGHTON MIFFLIN COMPANY
Evanston, Illinois • Boston • Dallas

ISBN-10: 0-618-88991-4

ISBN 978-0-618-88991-4

3 4 5 6 7 8 9 - PPN - 11 10 09 08

Contents

User's Guide and Answers

LATIN AMERICA: PHYSICAL GEOGRAPHY AND HISTORY

MEXICO

CONTENTS, *CONTINUED*

Transparencies

TO THE TEACHER

This overhead transparency book contains a variety of transparencies for each chapter in this unit of McDougal Littell *World Cultures and Geography.*

- Display the day's **Three-Minute Warm-Up** to focus students' attention as they enter class. A brief question or activity on each warm-up draws on prior knowledge, generates inferences and predictions, and awakens interest in the lesson ahead.
- Display the chapter's **World Art and Cultures** transparency to engage visual learners.
- Display the chapter's **Map Transparencies** to help students practice interpreting maps and for in-depth analysis of geography's impact on history.
- The **Essential Question** transparency with every chapter helps you review big ideas and summarize chapter content.
- The **User's Guide** for each transparency presents engaging discussion ideas, steps for modeling critical thinking, and an answer for every question.

TT1 Three-Minute Warm-Ups

Latin America: Physical Geography and History

Section 1

Mountains

Section 2

They are the world's longest and second highest range.

Section 3

Possible answer: They faced the difficulty of building roads through very rugged terrains.

Section 4

The direction of the exchange of products between North America and Europe

TT2 Essential Question

Latin America: Physical Geography and History

Answers

1. Sierra Madre Occidental; Sierra Madre Oriental; isthmus; Greater and Lesser Antilles; Tropic of Cancer; rivers in Mexico are too small to cross
2. Higher climates; Panama Canal is needed to bypass South America; much precipitation in Central America
3. Andes Mountains, Amazon River, rainforest, highlands
4. Has a variety of climates giving it many different types of vegetation
5. Olmec, Maya, Aztec, Inca
6. Olmec becomes cultural hearth; Olmec heads and Mayan pyramids left behind
7. Conquistador, Father Hidalgo, Simón Bolívar, José de San Martín
8. Spain's colonies in Latin America became independent
9. Possible answers: European languages like Spanish and Portuguese; different architectural styles and government

TT3 Critical Thinking

Latin America: Physical Geography and History

Section 1: Physical Geography of Mexico, Central America, and the Caribbean

Teaching Strategies

Use the diagram on transparency TT3 to categorize the physical geography of Mexico, Central America, and the Caribbean Islands. Ask students to identify an important physical feature of Mexico and Central America. (Possible answers: Mexico sits atop 3 tectonic plates, active volcanoes) What are some factors that affect the Caribbean climate? (Possible answers: Warm seas, wind)

Answers

Landforms

1. Mountains
2. Plateaus
3. Plains

Influences on Climate

1. Location in tropical zone
2. Elevation
3. Winds

Vegetation

1. Rain forests
2. Deciduous forests
3. Desert shrubs

TT4 Critical Thinking

Latin America: Physical Geography and History

Section 2: Physical Geography of South America

Teaching Strategies

Use the diagram on transparency TT4 to summarize features of South America's physical geography. Ask students what features of South America are the same as North America? (Possible answers: Mountains in the west, large river systems) What are some differences? (Possible answers: Abundant rain forests in South but not North America, arctic climates in North but not South America)

Answers

Landforms, Rivers, and Lakes

The Andes Mountains, including its valleys and the altiplano; South America is drained by five major river systems; few large natural lakes; the Central Plains include the llanos, Gran Chaco, Amazon rainforest, and pampas; Eastern Highlands include the Guiana Highlands and the Brazilian highlands

Climate and Vegetation

Mountain climate in Andes mountains; tropical climate in low latitudes; the rain forest climate is hot and wet with a variety of trees including rosewood, Brazil nut, rubber, mahogany, and cedar; rich soil of the grasslands produces a variety of crops, particularly soybeans and wheat; in desert fog zones, cacti, ferns and other vegetation grows

TT5 Critical Thinking

Latin America: Physical Geography and History

Section 3: Ancient Civilizations

Teaching Strategies

Use the diagram on transparency TT5 to compare and contrast the Aztec and Incan Empires. Ask students to identify ways in which the Aztec and Inca adapted to their surroundings. (Possible answers: Aztec, *chinampas*; Inca, terraced gardening) What is one similarity between the Olmec and Maya? (Possible answer: They both abandoned their cities for an unknown reason.)

Answers

Aztec Empire

in the valley of Mexico; strong military empire built through warfare; created water gardens called *chinampas* to grow food and flowers

Both

Ruled large empire; planned capital city; conquered by the Spanish

Inca Empire

In Andes Mountains, centered on the capital city of Cuzco; built roads; used quipus to keep records; cut terraces into the mountainsides to farm the steep lands; built aqueducts to farm

TT6 Critical Thinking

Latin America: Physical Geography and History

Section 4: From Colonization to Independence

Teaching Strategies

Use the diagram on transparency TT6 to record events that led to independence in Mexico and countries in South America. Ask students to identify occurrences in world history that helped inspire Central and South American colonies to fight for independence. (Possible answers: Napoleon's invasion of Europe distracted Spain from it colonies; The American and French Revolutions inspired others to want freedom.)

Answers

1521: Hernán Cortés defeats the Aztec.
1532: Francisco Pizarro defeats the Inca.
1810: Father Hidalgo calls for a rebellion against Spain. Bolívar and San Martín fight for South American independence.
1821: Mexico gains independence from Spain.
1822: Brazil gains independence from Portugal.
1826: All of Latin America (except Cuba and Puerto Rico) is independent.

TT7 Map

Latin America: Physical Geography and History

Latin America: Physical

Background

Latin America covers an enormous area, from the southern borders of the United States to the tip of Tierra del Fuego. The region contains highlands, lowlands, plains, rain forests, and deserts and is bounded by the Atlantic and Pacific oceans, the Caribbean Sea, and the Gulf of Mexico.

Mexico consists of a dry plateau, crossed by broad valleys and enclosed by the Sierra Nevada Mountains on either side. Baja California and the Yucatan Peninsula are the main low-lying areas. Central America is mountainous and forested. The Caribbean consists of three main island groups: the Bahamas and the Greater and Lesser Antilles.

Questions and Activities

1. Which large bodies of water surround Latin America? (Atlantic Ocean on the east, Pacific Ocean on the west, and the Gulf of Mexico and Caribbean Sea border Central America and the island groups)

2. Discuss the concept of a rain shadow and how mountains act as natural barriers to the flow of moist air. Ask how this explains some of the features of the South American landscape. (Possible answer: Parts of the pampas lie in the Andes's rain shadow. As a result, Patagonia contains an arid desert, and the Atacama Desert, squeezed between two mountain ranges, is one of the driest regions on Earth.)

3. What are the names of four South American rivers that flow into the Atlantic Ocean? What major lake is located on the border of Peru and Bolivia? (The Amazon, the Orinoco, the Araguaia, and the Rio de La Plata; Titicaca)

TT8 Map

Latin America: Physical Geography and History

Latin America: Political

Background

South America is divided into Spanish-speaking and Portuguese-speaking sections. This geographical division stems from the Treaty of Tordesilles, which split the continent between the colonial powers of Portugal and Spain. The conquest of Peru and Mexico paved the way for a vast Spanish colonial empire, while Portugal settled the Atlantic coast of the continent.

Central America connects North and South America. Mexico is the largest country occupying the Central American landmass. The Spanish ruled over the region for 300 years, unifying it with their language and religion.

The Caribbean countries are a chain of islands, settled and claimed by many European powers.

Questions and Activities

1. Which European nations still control land in Latin America? (United Kingdom, France, Netherlands)

2. Which Central American country has no coastline on the Caribbean? (El Salvador)

3. What Caribbean Island is located closest to the United States? Which island state is closest to Venezuela? (Bahamas; Trinidad and Tobago)

4. What two South American countries are completely landlocked? Which countries share land at the southern tip of the continent? (Paraguay and Bolivia; Chile and Argentina)

TT9 World Art and Cultures

Latin America: Physical Geography and History

Machu Picchu

Background

Machu Picchu was once a great city of the Inca. It demonstrates their extraordinary building and architectural skill. This astounding city, built at an altitude of 8,000 feet, is just one of a network of cities built by the Inca during the late 15th century.

The city had distinct parts. To the south of the city were extensive agricultural terraces. These terraces bordered the main entrance to the city and played a role in its defense.

To the north of the city was a dense residential area. This was in turn divided into two parts. One part was sometimes called the "noble quarter." Here were beautiful buildings of cut stone. In the other sector, which is shown in transparency TT9, were layers of buildings made of granite rubble and clay mortar. In this area was also a series of staggered fountains and canals. These were dug into the granite and formed a water supply and irrigation network. Other important parts of Machu Picchu included its main square and its royal mausoleum.

Questions and Activities

1. Ask students which parts of the architecture reflects the surroundings. (Some buildings have pointed tops like mountains, and others slope and conform to the mountains topography.)
2. Ask students to speculate on the climate. (Students might also speculate that it is generally cool at this altitude.)
3. **Cooperative Learning**
   Have students work together to speculate on the daily life activities of the people who occupied this site. (Students should list agricultural as well as religious/ceremonial activities. They should also suggest the making of clothing and shelter.)

TT10 World Art and Cultures

Latin America: Physical Geography and History

Monastery of San Francisco, Quito, Ecuador

Background

The Monastery of San Francisco was the first European church built in Quito, Ecuador. The city itself is built on the ruins of a former Incan capital, which was destroyed during the Spanish conquest. Quito is now a UNESCO World Heritage Site.

The church took nearly 80 years to complete. Construction began around 1534. Although the church was actually built by indigenous artisans, the architectural design is a mix of Renaissance and Baroque styles. The main church of the monastery is shown in transparency TT10.

The facade [the front section] of the church showcases the influence of European styles. The use of Doric columns on the first story and Ionic columns on the second story is an obvious European feature.

Indigenous influences are found in the interior of the church. For example, the gold leaf, or gilding, of the majority of the interior is of an Incan style. Also, suns that resemble human faces are frequently used as design elements within the church. These figures can be traced to indigenous religious movements.

Questions and Activities

1. How is the combination of styles used in the church similar to the overall culture of the Americas? (Possible answer: Both South and North American cultures contain a blending of indigenous and European influences.)
2. **Using a Search Engine**
   Find the website for UNESCO World Heritage Sites. Choose another World Heritage Site and learn more about it. Why has this site been preserved? What dangers exist for the preservation of your chosen site? Present your findings to the class.

TT11 Three-Minute Warm-Ups

Mexico

Section 1

Possible answer: more land, fairer wages, and better working conditions

Section 2

Possible answers: traditional and modern buildings and clothes; transportation by animal and car; ancient customs and modern sports

Section 3

Possible answers: to create better jobs and improve the standard of living; to generate more tax money to pay for improvements in poor areas

TT12 Essential Question

Mexico

Answers

1. Santa Anna becomes president of Mexico; Napoleon names Maximillian empreror; Francisco Madero starts a revolution; Vicente Fox elected president in 2000
2. Lower classes gain power in the constitution
3. Mexican independence, Mexican-American War, Mexican Revolution, new Constitution of 1917
4. Government is working to improve conditions in rural areas
5. Plaza of the Three Cultures; most people live in urban areas; Diego Rivera is a famous muralist
6. La Quinceañera, Day of the Dead, fútbol games
7. Mexico takes part in global economy; Mexico joins NAFTA
8. Maquiladoras; Mexico has become industrialized.
9. Mexico joins NAFTA.
10. Possible answers: A two-party system does promote democracy because one group of people will not always be in charge and parties can represent the interests of different groups.

TT13 Critical Thinking

Mexico

Section 1: A Struggle Toward Democracy

Teaching Strategies

Use the diagram on transparency TT13 to analyze the effects of the causes listed. Ask students to make an inference about why the Mexican economy was weak after independence. (Possible answer: As a colony, the Mexican economy was linked with or dependent upon its colonizer, Spain.)

Answers

Mexico and the U.S. could not agree.

War broke out between Mexico and the U.S. The war lasted two years.

New constitution

The constitution guaranteed freedom of speech and set up a federal system of government, but it did not make Catholicism the official religion.

Huge gap between rich and poor

Led to the Mexican Revolution

Constitution of 1917

Farmland was redistributed; brought about changes regarding workers' rights and the relationship between Church and state

TT14 Critical Thinking

Mexico

Section 2: A Blend of Traditions

Teaching Strategies

Use the diagram on transparency TT14 to summarize the main sections of Section 2. Ask students to identify a push factor that causes people to move to urban areas in Mexico. (Poor conditions in rural areas) What are some features of rural life in Mexico? (Possible answer: Villages, farms, dirt floors in houses, limited health care)

Answers

People and Lifestyle

Most Mexicans are *mestizos*; a blend of Indian, Spanish, and modern influences; most people live in urban areas; family life is very important

Mexico's Great Murals

Murals, huge paintings on sides of buildings, are an important art form; Mexican writers often write about the nation's social and political problems

Celebrations and Sports

Mexicans celebrate historical and religious holidays: Independence Day, *Cinco de Mayo*, Easter, and the Day of the Dead; soccer, baseball, bullfighting, and jai alai

TT15 Critical Thinking

Mexico

Section 3: Creating a New Economy

Teaching Strategies

Use the diagram on transparency TT15 to help find main ideas and supporting details about modern Mexico's economy. Ask students to evaluate whether or not a *maquiladora* is a good or bad thing for Mexico's economy. Why or why not? (Possible answer: *Maquiladoras* provide jobs but they make Mexico's economy dependent on other countries. Any supported answer is acceptable.)

Answers

Takes bigger role in global economy

Maquiladoras assemble imported materials into finished goods for export.

Increases its industries

Mexico has become a major producer of crude petroleum.

Signed NAFTA

Mexico signed the North American Free Trade Agreement (NAFTA) with the United States and Canada.

Struggle to reduce pollution

Mexico has urged automobile manufacturers to produce cars that use cleaner fuels.

TT16 Map

Mexico

Mexico: Political

Background

Mexico is a federal republic. There are 31 states and a federal district like Washington, D.C. in the United States. Mexico's federal district includes Mexico City, the capital. Mexico's largest river, the Rio Grande, actually forms part of its northern border with the United States. That border area is sometimes the source of tension between Mexico and the United States.

The Yucatán Peninsula that juts into the Gulf of Mexico includes the Mexican states of Campeche, Yucatán, and Quintana Roo, and the nations of Belize and Guatemala. Mexico and Guatemala have had disputes over land along their borders.

Questions and Activities

1. Point out Baja California, Tijuana, and Ciudad Juaréz. These places have large concentrations of *maquiladoras*. Why are these cities prime locations for *maquiladoras*? (*Maquiladoras* produce goods for export to other countries, including the United States. The location of these cities on the U.S. border means they can easily transport goods to a major importer.)
2. Which Mexican states border the United States? (Baja California, Sonora, Chihuahua, Coahuila, Nuevo Léon, Tamaulipas)
3. Which Mexican states share the border with Guatemala in the south? (Chiapas, Tabasco, Campeche, Quintana Roo)

TT17 Map
Mexico
Mexico: Population Density

Background
Mexico has large areas of sparse population. This is due, in part, to the climate and in part to geography. Deserts in the northwest are thinly populated, as is Baja California and the northern portion of the Mexican plateau. But other regions that may be more hospitable, such as the Yucatan Peninsula, have simply had little road or rail access until recent years. Most Mexicans live in the Mexican Plateau, an area that runs roughly down the middle of the country.

Approximately 70 percent of Mexicans live in cities. The map shows that Mexico City and other border cities are big population centers. The border cities of Tijuana and Ciudad Juarez have high populations due to the increase in *maquiladoras* since the signing of NAFTA. Mexicans move from rural areas to cities like these to find work.

The city of Monterrey, located in the northeastern part of Mexico, benefits from being situated near a river. In 1882, a railroad to Laredo, Texas, brought foreign investment. Then, the Inter-American Highway, which links North and South America, triggered another boom.

Questions and Activities
1. Mexico has few major rivers. Which city is on the Rio Grande? (Ciudad Juárez)
2. Look at the strip of heavy density in the middle of the country. What role might geography play in this density? (The area must have physical traits that make living there more hsopitable.)
3. What is the population density of the region that includes Léon? Ciudad Juarez? Tijuana? (All are over 250 persons per square mile)

TT18 World Art and Cultures
Mexico
Charro (cowboy)

Background
The *charrería* is an important sport in Mexico and is sometimes called the national sport. A *charrería* is much like an American rodeo. *Charros*, or cowboys, compete in it. Although women compete in certain parts of the *charrería*, it is primarily a male sport.

In any ranching culture, roping and riding skills are not only admired but also vital to economic existence. The *charrería* became popular on the large *haciendas*, or ranches, of Mexico during the 19th century. These events celebrated the roundups and the *herraderos* (brandings).

Note the wrangler's traditional cowboy dress. Note that, in many *charrerías*, much more ornate and festive clothing is worn. Note how the *charro* has perfect control not only over his rope, but also over his horse.

Questions and Activities
1. The cowboy's rope has been swung to create a lasso. Use classroom dictionaries to have students look up the etymology of the word *lasso*. (*Lasso* comes from the Spanish word *lazo* with the same meaning.)
2. The geographic theme of movement can be seen in the borrowings of one language from another. English has many words related to horses and horse riding that came to it from Spanish. Have students research the origins of other words related to those topics. (Other words may include mustang, lariat, and bronco.)
3. **Cooperative Learning**
   Have students name the visible parts of the cowboy's apparel and speculate on purposes for each. (The broad brimmed hat keeps dust out of the cowboy's face and shades him from the sun. Chaps are worn over ordinary pants to protect the cowboys legs.)

TT19 World Art and Cultures

Mexico

Frida Kahlo (1907–1954)

Background

Frida Kahlo was one of the great and prolific Mexican artists of the first half of the 20th century. She is best known for her self-portraits, in which she often features her own severe, dramatic face amid fruit and flowers. In her painting, as in her life, she seemed to identify with the Mexican peasant, though she herself came from a bourgeois family. Her paintings often share motifs and colors with Mexican folk art; in some of them, she cultivated a certain naïve look. In others she expressed the popular surrealistic images of her times.

In *El camion* [The Bus], an early painting of 1929, Kahlo used oil on canvas to present six passengers who represent different walks of life. Students might realize that most notable among them are two figures who are opposites. One is the blue-eyed capitalist, his bag of money held confidently in hand. The opposite figure is barefoot peasant woman with her bundle representing poverty or manual labor.

Questions

1. Ask students to pay careful attention to clothing and other details in order to suggest the identities of the other passengers. (From left to right: The first woman is perhaps of the middle or working class; she has on shoes of a working woman. Next to her is a laborer, representative of the working class. The woman on the far right with a more stylish clothing and a trim figure, suggests the upper class.)

2. Ask students to describe the scene shown outside the bus windows. (It is mostly agricultural, but there is a new encroachment of industry, as represented by the smokestacks.) How does the exterior scene symbolize changes in Mexican life? (Mexico is changing from an agricultural nation to an industrialized nation.)

TT20 Three-Minute Warm-Ups

Middle America and Spanish-Speaking South America

Section 1

Possible answer: It allows people to see a wide area and be closer to wildlife in the trees. It's less harmful to the environment than building a road through the forest.

Section 2

Possible answer: These islands have nice beaches and a warm climate.

Section 3

Possible answer: Alike—both modern-looking cities; different—Bogotá seems to be at a higher elevation than Caracas

Section 4

Advantages: good for coffee growing, mining, raising llamas and alpacas; Disadvantages: difficult for farming and transportation

Section 5

Possible answer: Both ride on horses to herd large numbers of animals.

TT21 Essential Question

Middle America and Spanish-speaking South America

Answers

1. Most countries, until recently, have been dictatorships.
2. Ecotourism, subsistence farming, *maquiladoras*, CAFTA
3. Blend of Spanish, Indian, and African; most Central Americans are mestizos; artisans make things with their hands
4. Independence movements occurred in early 1900's; Puerto Rico is commonwealth of the United States; Cuba is communist.
5. One-crop economy, tourism
6. Taino were indigenous; variety of languages; music reflects a blend of cultures
7. Simón Bolívar leads independence for Venezuela and Colombia. Dictators to federal republic
8. Venezuela: oil; Colombia: coffee and agricultural products
9. Joropo; most Venezuelans live in cities; Colombian artists: Gabriel García Márquez, Fernando Botero
10. Peru, Bolivia, and Ecuador are republics; struggled with democracy
11. Peru: unstable, too mountainous for farming, tourism; Bolivia: natural gas; Ecuador: petroleum
12. *Mestizos* and indigenous people; languages: Spanish, native languages Quechua and Aymara
13. José de San Martín helped Argentina and Chile gain independence.
14. Gauchos play an important role; *estancias*; service industries
15. Large urban populations; dances: the tango
16. Possible answer: It makes them more dependent because if tourists from other countries do not visit, then a part of their economy collapses.

TT22 Critical Thinking

Middle America and Spanish-Speaking South America

Section 1: Central America

Teaching Strategies

Use the diagram on transparency TT22 to categorize the major aspects of Central America's government, economy, and culture. Ask students to identify one thing most Central American countries have in common. (Possible answer: All the countries except Costa Rica have struggled with democracy for many years; gap between rich and poor)

Answers

Government

Costa Rica is the only South American country that has been a democracy since the 1900s; most Central American countries are democracies but have struggled since gaining independence; the wealthy control most aspects of the government in other countries.

Economy

Most agriculture consists of subsistence farming; ecotourism is a major industry; developing technology and telecommunication industries; signers of CAFTA; the Panama Canal is important to world trade.

Culture

Population is one-half urban; family is important; known for works of artisans; music combines traditional sounds with modern rhythms; calypso, salsa, and punta rock are popular; Spanish is the official language everywhere except Belize; most people are Roman Catholics.

TT23 Critical Thinking

Middle America and Spanish-Speaking South America

Section 2: The Caribbean

Teaching Strategies

Use the diagram on transparency TT23 to summarize information about the economies, governments, and cultures of the Caribbean islands. Discuss the disadvantages of a one-crop economy. (Possible answers: Market prices or a natural disaster could ruin the entire economy of a nation.)

Answers

Economy

Sugar cane is the most important product; sugar crop declined so fruit and other crops were developed; many nations are diversifying their economies—mining and tourism; some nations belong to the Caribbean Community and Common Market (CARICOM)

Government

Most nations were European colonies; most nations are independent; most nations have democratically elected governments; Puerto Rico is a commonwealth of the United States; Cuba is a communist country.

Culture

Cultures of the Caribbean islands have been influenced by European, African, and native Indian cultures; Spanish, French, and English are spoken; music reflects the musical styles of Spain, Africa, and the Caribbean; steel drum is popular; festivals, such as Carnival, and soccer are popular forms of entertainment; most live in urban areas.

TT24 Critical Thinking

Middle America and Spanish-Speaking South America

Section 3: Venezuela and Colombia

Teaching Strategies

Use the diagram on transparency TT24 to record details about Venezuela and Colombia. Ask students how Venezuela's dependence on oil for its economy is similar to a one-crop economy. (The entire economy can fall prey to factors outside the country's control, like fluctuating oil prices.)

Answers

Government

Venezuela: former Spanish colony; once ruled by dictators; federal republic

Columbia: former Spanish colony; civil war continues to today; republic; legislative, executive and judicial branches

Economy

Venezuela: leading oil exporter, dependent on oil production; half of farmers cultivate small farms; large farms and ranches supply commercial products.

Columbia: relies on agricultural products; coffee is leading legal export; cut flowers alternative to illegal cocaine production; manufacturing and service industries important; leader in emerald mining

People

Venezuela: most are mestizos; Spanish official language; most are Roman Catholics; most live in cities; sports, music, and dancing

Columbia: Spanish official language; most are Roman Catholics; most live in cities; rich culture, including writer Gabriel García Márquez

TT25 Critical Thinking

Middle America and Spanish-Speaking South America

Section 4: Peru, Bolivia, and Ecuador

Teaching Strategies

Use the diagram on transparency TT25 to categorize details about Peru, Bolivia, and Ecuador. Ask students to identify similarities between the three countries. (Possible answers: all are former Spanish colonies; populations are mixed; many natural resources)

Answers

Peru

Government: once Spanish colony; experienced military takeovers; democratic republic today

Economy: one-third of people are farmers; petroleum, minerals, fish, and food crops

People: most are *mestizos*; African, Asian, and European; Spanish and Quechua are official languages; most live in urban areas; create sculpture and pottery

Bolivia

Government: once Spanish colony; experienced dictatorships; now democratic republic

Economy: developing resources; llamas and alpacas, natural gas, coffee, and food crops

People: Spanish, Quechua, and Aymara are official languages; farmers, artisans; *mestizos*

Ecuador

Government: once Spanish colony; experienced dictatorships; now democratic republic

Economy: developing resources; petroleum and gold

People: Indians; *mestizos*; artisans

TT26 Critical Thinking

Middle America and Spanish-Speaking South America

Section 5: The Southern Cone

Teaching Strategies

Use the diagram on transparency TT26 to organize details about a nation's history and government, economy, and population. Ask students to identify which country is more influenced by European culture. (Argentina) Why might this be? (About 85 percent of the population is of European descent, unlike other nations that have larger *mestizo* populations.)

Answers

Argentina

History and Government: Once Spanish colony; controlled by dictators until 1990; republic today
Economy: Service industries employ more than half of workers; beef, cattle, grains, fishing; petroleum
Population: Large urban population; 85 percent European ancestry; gauchos and tango

Paraguay

History and Government: Once Spanish colony; now constitutional republic
Economy: Wood products are important industries.
Population: The Guaraní are the nation's largest indigenous group.

Chile

History and Government: Once Spanish colony; General Augusto Pinochet ruled as military dictator from 1973 until 1990.
Economy: Chile developed copper mining and fishing industries.
Population: Mostly *mestizo*

Uruguay

History and Government: Once Spanish colony; now constitutional republic.
Economy: More than 60 percent of people work in service industries.
Population: Most people are of Spanish and Italian ancestry. Culture is influenced more by European traditions.

TT27 Map

Middle America and Spanish-Speaking South America

Caribbean Islands: Political

Background

Christopher Columbus' first landfall in the Americas occurred in the Caribbean islands. The actual location of his first landfall is not certain, but the island of San Salvador in the Bahamas is a commonly accepted spot. Wherever he landed first, his arrival dramatically shaped the islands. The Spanish colonialists that followed soon enslaved the indigenous populations of most islands. Disease and overwork killed the slaves as they toiled to send resources back to colonial masters.

Haiti and the Dominican Republic occupy an island commonly known as Hispaniola. Columbus landed here, as well. Hispaniola provided many resources to Spain, but then part of the island fell under the influence of French pirates. In the 17th century, a treaty between France and Spain gave the western portion to France — now known as Haiti.

Cuba is the largest island in the Caribbean. Just 90 miles from the U.S., it has been the focal point of many events. The United States tried to buy Cuba in the 19th century, and it helped Cuba in its fight for independence from Spain. Into the 20th century, the United States had many financial ties to the island. That all ended when Fidel Castro took power in 1959 and turned the nation into a communist country. The United States still maintains a naval base at Guantánamo Bay.

Questions and Activities

1. What are the two countries that occupy one island? What are their capitals? (Haiti, whose capital is Port au Prince; Dominican Republic, whose capital is Santo Domingo)
2. What is the capital of Cuba? Why would the U.S. be especially interested in the politics and government of this nation? (Havana; Cuba is only 90 miles away)
3. Which island nation is located off the east coast of the United States? (Bahamas)

TT28 Map

Middle America and Spanish-Speaking South America

Argentina: Economic Activities

Background

Argentina is an economic leader in Latin America. The service industry is the top sector there. But livestock and agriculture, two historically important areas, are still a large part of the economy.

Argentina is the second largest producer of cattle in Latin America, behind Brazil. The Pampas, in the south central portion of the country, is the main cattle raising area. Much of that beef stays in the country. Argentina is also a world leader in the production of wool. Raising crops is found largely in the north. Soybeans and corn top the list of exports, but wheat is the biggest crop overall.

Despite Argentina's long coastline, the fishing industry isn't overwhelmingly prominent. Argentines prefer beef to seafood. However, seafood exports are still important. Manufacturing, mainly around Buenos Aires, is also significant — especially the processing of agricultural resources.

Questions and Activities

1. What agricultural resources are most important to the Pampas region of Argentina? (Corn and wheat)
2. Which cities count meatpacking and food processing as important industries? (Rosario, Buenos Aires, La Plata, Bahía Blanca)
3. Why would the location of Buenos Aires be good for manufacturing and industry? (Possible answer: Buenos Aires is on a bay and has access to the Atlantic for shipping.)
4. What resources and land use are found in Patagonia? (Livestock raising, metals)

TT29 World Art and Cultures

Middle America and Spanish-Speaking South America

Andean Textiles

Background

Handmade clothing in the Andes is characterized by its warmth and its brightly colored beauty. Handmade items are often woven; sometimes, they are knitted. In either case, they are often made from the wool of the sheep that graze the mountainsides. Sometimes, they are made from alpaca or llama hair.

The woman shown in TT29 wears traditional dress. The wrapped textiles shown on the shoulders and back of the woman serve many purposes. In it women can carry a small child, food, or other items.

Note that the woman wears two layers of outerwear. Although she is wearing a manufactured sweater, she could just as easily be wearing poncho or an *ira*, a garment that is cut like a poncho but with sides sewn up to the armholes. On the women's head is a bowler-style hat. These hats are often made of felted sheep's wool and adorned with a hatband.

Questions and Activities

1. Ask what the women's dress suggests about her daily life. (She needs warmth in layers. She probably carries things from place to place on her back. The woven items are not just practical but beautiful, so the culture prizes beauty in its textiles. Manufactured goods are available.)

2. Ask students to speculate on the climate. (The Andean highlands are often chilly; wool is a necessity for warmth.)

3. **Using the Internet**
   Have students work together to research the various clothing items worn by the Andeans.

TT30 World Art and Cultures

Middle America and Spanish-Speaking South America

Dancing the Tango

Background

The tango falls into the category of social dances. Many social dances are performed with variations of the closed and half-open positions. The tango is performed almost exclusively in closed or half-open positions, or slight modifications of them. The couple shown in this photograph are in the closed position: partners face each other, with the woman slightly to the man's right. The man holds the woman's right hand with his left hand and puts his other hand on her waist. She puts her left hand on his right shoulder. The half-open position is much the same, except that the partners are side by side, and the woman stands to the man's right

The man is performing an extremely characteristic step called a dip. Explain that all the movements of tango are stylized. The positions lead to sudden hesitations that may include dips, leans, and even a backward-flung head movement. Tango dancers move elegantly and rapidly, stop as if to pause for a photo, and then resume their dramatic movement.

Questions and Activities

1. Ask students to name a social dance they or friends know and to tell how it differs from what they see here.

2. Have students comment on how the dress of these dancers reflects what they have learned about the tango. (The dancers' dress is both formal and dramatic, like the tango itself.)

3. **Cooperative Learning**
   Have students work together to find out about tango music. Students should describe the instruments, the tempo, and rhythms of the tango. (The tempo would have to vary, with variations from relatively quick to stopped movement The rhythm of the tango is typically one-two-three-and-four. Big band instruments might play the music.)

TT31 Three-Minute Warm-Ups

Brazil

Section 1

Possible answer: The city is built between the ocean and the mountains. It doesn't have a lot of room to expand outward, so it has a lot of skyscrapers.

Section 2

Roots: African, European, Asian, and Indian; Examples: African influences on religion, food, and the arts; Indian influence on the arts

Section 3

Possible answers: Rivers provide a major source of Brazil's electric power.

TT32 Essential Question

Brazil

Answers

1. Pedro Álvares Cabral, Dom Pedro I, Dom Pedro II
2. Rio de Janeiro, Portugal, *favelas*, Brasília
3. Treaty of Tordesillas
4. Immigrants, Candomblé/West African, natives, Oscar Niemeyer
5. *Quilombos*, National Congress Building
6. Carnival
7. Amazon natives, farmers
8. Amazon, the rainforest
9. Brazil declares rainforest a protected area
10. Possible answer: Try not to purchase products from the rainforest. Plant trees to replenish what has been lost to deforestation.

TT33 Critical Thinking

Brazil

Section 1: From Portuguese Colony to Modern Giant

Teaching Strategies

Use the diagram on transparency TT33 to show major events in Brazil's history. Ask students how Brazil, also begun as a colony, has a similar history to the other countries of South America. (Possible answers: Portugal, like Spain, took many natural resources from Brazil. Brazil struggled with democracy.)

Answers

1. 1494: Spain and Portugal sign the Treaty of Tordesillas, giving Portugal control lands east of the line.
2. 1500: Cabral claims Brazil for Portugal.
3. 1822: Brazil declares independence from Portugal.
4. 1831: Dom Pedro II becomes emperor of Brazil.
5. 1889: Brazil becomes a constitutional republic.
6. 1891: Brazil adopts a new constitution based on the U.S. constitution.
7. 1985: Military rule ends.
8. 1988: A constitution establishes the present-day government.

TT34 Critical Thinking

Brazil

Section 2: A Multicultural Society

Teaching Strategies

Use the diagram on transparency TT34 to categorize details about Brazilian people and culture. Discuss how Brazilian culture is similar to the United States. (Possible answer: Like the U.S., Brazil's culture is a mixture of many cultural influences.)

Answers

Art and Architecture

1. Crafts made by Brazil's Indian groups
2. Important sculptors and muralists
3. Famous architect, Niemeyer

Music

1. Blends African, European, and Indian cultures
2. Samba is the most famous Brazilian music.
3. Different kinds of drums create unique rhythms; samba, bossa nova, and capoeira

Entertainment

1. Carnival
2. Beaches
3. Sports, particularly football (soccer)

TT35 Critical Thinking

Brazil

Section 3: Developing an Abundant Land

Teaching Strategies

Use the diagram on transparency TT35 to organize ideas about Brazil's economy. Ask students to brainstorm ways to expand Brazil's economy without cutting down the rain forests. (Possible answer: Ecotourism is a good way to use the rain forests for economic gain without destroying them.)

Answers

Size of Economy

Largest economy in South America; one of the world's largest

Resources

Abundance of natural resources; large deposits of iron, manganese, and bauxite; major producer of gold and diamonds; hydroelectricity supplies energy needed to run industries

Industry

Brazil has invested in high-tech equipment to run its manufacturing industries; world leader in automobile production

Agriculture

One-fifth of Brazil's workers are employed in agriculture; largest producer of sugar cane, coffee, and leading exporter of agricultural products

TT36 Map

Brazil

Resources of Brazil

Background

The south and southeast are the main economic centers of Brazil. The nation has long been a mining leader. During colonial times under Portugal, and even after, Brazil's economy relied on one or two resources. In the 20th century, the economy diversified.

The state of São Paulo, in the southeast, has a large mechanized agriculture sector. Coffee, a leading agricultural product for Brazil, is important here. Other important commercial agricultural products include sugarcane, cotton, bananas, and oranges. Livestock includes hogs, sheep, and horses. The area is a major manufacturing center in the world, turning the nation's abundant iron, manganese, and bauxite supply into finished goods.

The most obvious and abundant resource in Brazil is the Amazon rain forest. It is rich in raw materials. Rubber and timber are major resources, along with nuts and other fibers. Another resource of the forest is land — the forest is being cleared at an alarming rate to provide agricultural land. Nearly 20 percent of the forest has been cut down in the last 40 years. The growing cattle industry and soybean farmers consume a large amount of land through slash and burn deforestation. Finding a way to use the Amazon rain forest without destroying it is a major challenge for Brazil in the 21st century.

Questions and Activities

1. Where are the deposits of iron ore found in Brazil? (In the southeast and the northeast)
2. What type of land use borders the rain forest to the southeast? (Livestock raising and commercial agriculture)
3. Ask students if they think the Amazon rain forest can withstand the pressure from livestock raising and commercial agriculture. (Possible answer: It depends on whether people can find other types of work to do.)

TT37, TT37a Map

Brazil

Natural Resources and Rain Forests of Latin America

Background

The main map illustrates where several natural resources are found and the location of rain forests. Latin America is rich in natural resources. These range from minerals such as gold, silver, and precious gemstones, as well as energy resources such as petroleum and natural gas. In addition, the region produces abundant agricultural products and forest resources.

Mexico has major deposits of petroleum along its coast on the Gulf of Mexico. Oil also contributes to the economies of Venezuela, Ecuador, and Peru. Brazil has an industrial economy supported by mineral resources such as iron, aluminium, and copper. In contrast, mainland Central America, which is heavily forested, is relatively poor in resources.

The overlay map shows the original extent of Latin America's rain forests. Not only is the Amazon region unmatched in species diversity, but it is also a rich source of natural products. Among these forest products are rubber, chicle for chewing gum, timber, and quinine—a drug that fights malaria. Only a tiny fraction of forest plants have been studied for their possible medical benefits.

As the overlay shows, more and more of the Amazon rain forest is being destroyed. Logging kills wildlife and leads to erosion and flooding.

Questions and Activities

1. In which parts of Latin America do you find the largest areas of rain forest? (The Amazon Basin and parts of mainland Central America)
2. Why might developing nations be tempted to clear these forests? (Possible answers: industries that need raw materials, timber for buildings, and grazing land for cattle)
3. Where are major deposits of petroleum found? (Mexico, Venezuela, Peru, Ecuador, and the southern tip of South America)

TT38 World Art and Cultures

Brazil

Carnival

Background

Carnival is an event celebrated the world over. One common feature—whether it's Fasching in Germany or Mardi Gras in the United States—is that Carnival is a last celebration of excess before the Christian season of Lent.

Shown here is a Carnival float, one of many that might parade down the streets of Rio de Janeiro under the eyes of judges. Dancers, singers, and drummers follow. But the samba is perhaps the most distinctive characteristic of Carnival in Brazil. Like many things Brazilian, samba music is a mixture of European and African influences. The groups parading through Rio de Janeiro are known as samba schools (*escolas de samba*). First formed in 1928, samba schools are now social clubs important to the community in which they're based.

Carnival differs in other parts of Brazil. In the north, Carnival is more of an informal street festival. In Rio de Janeiro, Carnival is more formal and has been dominated by the upper classes. Either way, the streets fill with revelers before the Christian observance of Ash Wednesday.

Questions and Activities

1. What are some names for Carnival around the world? (Fasching in Germany, Mardi Gras in the United States)
2. How is Mardi Gras similar to Carnival? (Possible answer: Mardi Gras comes from a mixture of cultures and has elaborate parades.)
3. Research different Brazilian musical styles such as Batuque, Bossa Nova, or Tropicália. Bring recordings to class. Or, ask students to seek musicians and find recordings. Famous Brazilian musicians include Antonio Carlos Jobim, João Gilberto, and Caetano Veloso.

TT39 World Art and Cultures

Brazil

Statue of Christ the Redeemer, Rio de Janeiro

Background

The Statue of Christ the Redeemer, one of the most famous landmarks in the world, overlooks Rio de Janeiro from its perch atop Mount Corcovado. The mountain is named after its shape—"humpback."

As far back as 1859, leaders felt the top of Mount Corcovado would make an impressive site for a statue. The first proposal was a tribute to Brazil's Princess Isabel. The proposal for the present statue came in 1921. Planners decided that commissioning a monument to Jesus would also be a fitting tribute to the 100th anniversary of Brazilian independence in 1922.

In 1922, a foundation stone was laid, and 1931 saw the monument inaugurated. The chosen material for the statue was soapstone. Even though this type of rock can scratch easily, it can better withstand cracking caused by extreme weather. Nevertheless, efforts to restore the statue began in 2000 and have since been completed.

Questions and Activities

1. Looking at the photo shown here, why do you think the statue needed to be restored? (Possible answer: The statue is high atop a mountain and exposed to the elements. Wind, rain, and the humid climate could all affect the statue.)

2. Why do you think the statue was placed on top of Mount Corcovado? (The statue would be able to be seen all over the city and observed by ships coming into the port.)

Latin America

Transparencies